TE

Mario
Castelnuovo-Tedesco

SONATINA

for Flute and Guitar

OP. 205

Mauro
Giuliani

SERENATA

for Flute and Guitar

OP. 127

MUSIC MINUS ONE

SUGGESTIONS FOR USING THIS MMO EDITION

WE HAVE TRIED to create a product that will provide you an easy way to learn and perform these duets with a full accompaniment in the comfort of your own home. Because it involves a fixed performance, there is an inherent lack of flexibility in tempo and cadenza length. The following MMO features and techniques will reduce these inflexibilities and help you maximize the effectiveness of the MMO practice and performance system:

Where the soloist begins a movement *solo*, we have provided an introductory measure with subtle taps inserted at the actual tempo before the soloist's entrance.

Chapter stops on your CD are conveniently located throughout the piece at the beginnings of practice sections, and are cross-referdenced in the score. This should help you quickly find a desired place in the music as you learn the piece.

We have observed generally accepted tempi, but some may wish to perform at a different tempo, or to slow down or speed up the accompaniment for practice purposes. You can purchase from MMO specialized CD players which allow variable speed while maintaining proper pitch. This is an indispensable tool for the serious musician and you may wish to look into purchasing this useful piece of equipment for full enjoyment of all your MMO editions.

We want to provide you with the most useful practice and performance accompaniments possible. If you have any suggestions for improving the MMO system, please feel free to contact us. You can reach us by e-mail at *info@musicminusone.com.*

Music Minus One

3365

CONTENTS

MARIO CASTELNUOVO-TEDESCO
SONATINA
op. 205

MAURO GIULIANI
SERENATA
op. 127

ISBN 1-59615-341-5

Timeless Music from Disparate Times: Two Legendary Composers

MARIO CASTELNUOVO-TEDESCO was born in Firenze (Florence), Italy on 3 April 1895. His flair for the piano and for composition were obvious early on, and he was enrolled in the Cherubini Institute in Florence while quite young. He attained early attention with impressionistic, pastoral works such as *Cipressi*, originally written for piano in 1921 and scored for symphonic orchestra that same year. In 1933 his *I profeti* (Violin Concerto No. 2) was premiered with much fanfare by the New York Philharmonic with Jascha Heifitz as soloist under Toscanini's baton. In 1935, his Cello Concerto was premiered by the same ensemble with Piatigorsky as soloist.

Because of his Jewish heritage and the impending war in Europe, he emigrated with his family from Europe to the U.S. in 1939, with the help of both Toscanini and Heifitz. There he performed the premiere of his Second Piano Concerto under John Barbirolli's baton in New York.

He ultimately settled in Beverly Hills, California, where he served as composer on films such as *Tortilla Flat* (1942), *Gaslight* (1944) and *A Double Life* (1947, on which he collaborated with Miklos Rosza). He continued to prolifically compose many acclaimed works for the operatic stage; a cycle of overtures on Shakespearean themes; many works for solo instruments, chamber ensembles, symphonic orchestras and concerted works. He also taught such lauded latter-day film composers as André Previn, Henry Mancini and John Williams.

But it was the guitar for which Castelnuovo-Tedesco had his most durable affinity, and such great artists as Andrés Segovia regularly commissioned works from this great twentieth-century composer. Though he didn't play the instrument, his refined, delicate and nuanced style meshed perfectly with the gentle and distinct qualities of the guitar, and his orchestrations in the guitar concerti also reflect this delicacy of style. All in all, he wrote two concerti for solo guitar and orchestra, and one concerto for two guitars; plus a *Serenade* for guitar and chamber orchestra. His solo guitar music includes a guitar sonata and other shorter works such as the *Capriccio Diabolico* (a tribute to famed violinist Niccolò Paganini), *Caprichos de Goya* and many others.

Castelnuovo-Tedesco died in Beverly Hills on 15 March 1968. Much of his music remains unpublished, and his family subsequently made a large donation of his manuscripts and other effects to the Library of Congress, where they now reside.

MAURO GIULIANI remains unquestionably the most renowned Italian guitarist and one of the greatest guitar virtuosi the world has ever known. The quality and durability of his compositions speak for themselves.

He was born 27 July 1781 in the small town of Bisceglie in the southern Italian province of Bari—and not, as had long been supposed, in 1780 in Naples or Bologna. His early years defy thorough documentation, but it is now generally accepted that in his youth he studied the violoncello, with a thorough theoretical background in counterpoint. At some point early on, the six-string guitar became his principal instrument. His subsequent brilliance on this instrument makes clear that this was a fortuitous match for young Mauro's musical sensibility.

Soon after reaching adulthood in the early years of the 19th century, Giuliani came to recognize that, despite his undeniable talent, public interest in Italy for the guitar was dwarfed—as it was for almost all instrumental music—by the overwhelming national passion for opera. Giuliani joined what amounted to an exodus of talented Italian guitarists. He moved north, out of the country, to make a living. In 1806 he settled in Vienna.

The inordinately musically sophisticated Viennese population had a great appreciation for the guitar and its music. But just as Giuliani found a more appreciative public, he also found a greater amount of talented competition. Soon, however, Giuliani soared above the rest, including the two most established masters of the guitar in Vienna—Alois Wolf and Simon Molitor. If Vienna was at this time unchallenged as the musical capital of the world, Giuliani had undoubtedly become the world's greatest living guitarist.

More importantly for his posthumous legacy, Giuliani also became known as a brilliant composer for his instrument. In April 1808 he himself performed to considerable acclaim his first guitar concerto, opus 30 (which was, however, not published until 1810). By all accounts this performance solidified his already considerable position in Vienna, and it helped establish his reputation in the greater musical world as well. From this point on, Giuliani became the undisputed leader of the classical guitar movement in Vienna.

The height of his standing at this time is amply demonstrated by his being named *virtuoso onorario di camera* to Napoleon's second wife, the Empress Marie-Louise, a Hapsburg who resided in Vienna. And Giuliani moved in the realm of the musical aristocracy as well, performing for and with such brilliant musical Olympians as Beethoven, Diabelli, Hummel, Salieri and Haydn. At the premiere of Beethoven's Seventh Symphony, alongside Vienna's top musical elite, Giuliani played in the orchestra (on the violoncello, it is assumed, an instrument he evidently never entirely abandoned), and was publicly thanked by Beethoven in the press for his efforts. And he composed a great deal during this period—his total life's work amounts to many hundreds of compositions, including technical exercises which even today are considered *de rigeur* for all classical guitar students—all the while managing to continue performing and teaching.

But, as with so many genuine artists in any medium, talent rarely guarantees lengthy happiness or financial stability. Giuliani found himself in considerable debt, and in 1819 he left Vienna. He returned to his native Italy, living several years in Rome and finally settling in Naples. In his remaining years Giuliani again became patronized by the nobility, this time by that of the Neapolitan court. He died on 8 May 1829, not yet forty-eight years old.

—*Douglas Scharmann*

SONATINA
for Flute and Guitar
Op. 205

Mario Castelnuovo-Tedesco
(1895-1968)

MMO 3365

II.

2 12 *Four taps precede music*

Tempo di Siciliana (Andantino grazioso e malinconico)

III. Scherzo - Rondo

12

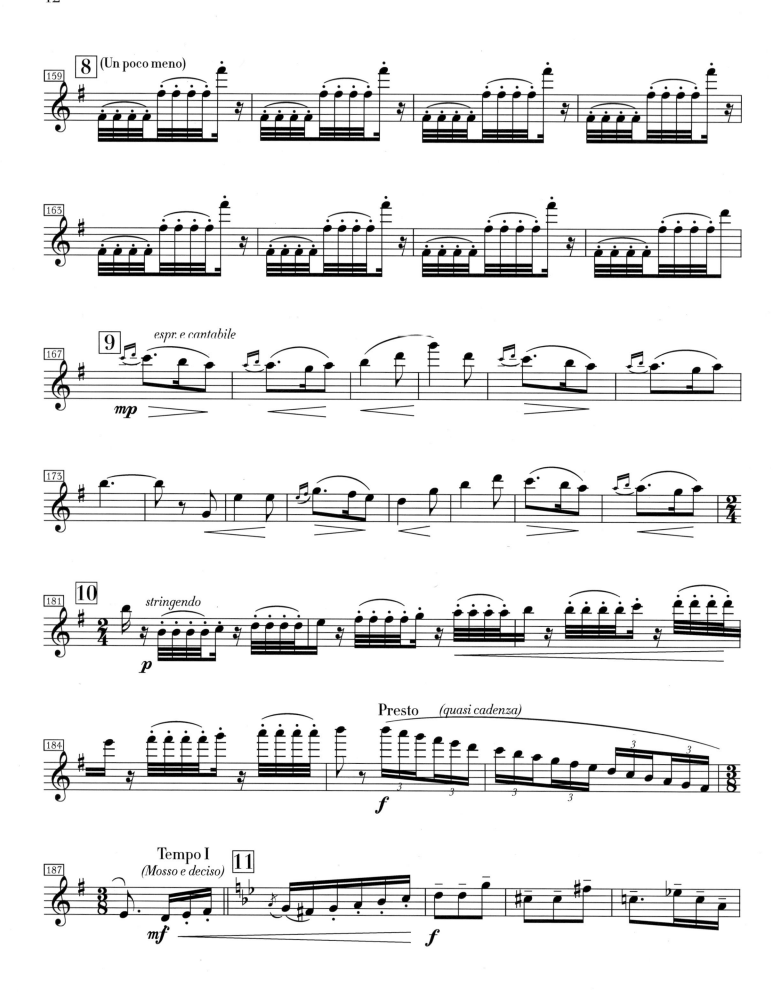

SERENATA

for Flute and Guitar

op. 127

Edited by Katarzyna Bury

Mauro Giuliani
(1781 - 1829)

Maestoso

FLUTE

II. Minuetto

Variazion II
Più lento

8 18 *Three taps precede music*

Variazion III
Primo tempo

IV. Rondo

9 19 *1-1/2 measures of taps (3 taps) precede music*

FLUTE CLASSICS

MUSIC MINUS ONE

Chamber Classics

J.S. BACH Sonata No. 1 in B minor /KUHLAU 2 Duets (2-CD Set) MMO CD 3344
J.S. Bach *Sonata No. 1 in B minor, BWV1030;* **Kuhlau** *Duet Sonata No. 1 in E minor, op. 10; Duet Sonata No. 2 in D major*

CASTELNUOVO-TEDESCO Sonatina; GIULIANI Serenata (2-CD Set) MMO CD 3365

Dances of Three Centuries MMO CD 3360
Ammerbach, Elias Nikolaus Orgel oder Instrument Tabulatur (1571-83): *Passamezzo;* **Anonymous** *Ora Baila Tu (Spanish Carnival Dance), c. 1500; Polish Dance;* **Attaingnant** The Cancionero Musical: *Gaillarde;* **J.G. Bohm** Rigaudon (from Suite in D): *Rigaudon (from Suite in D);* **Bull** The Fitzwilliam Virginal Book: *The Spanish Paven;* **Chambonnieres** Gigue (Canon) from 'Pieces deClavecin': *Gigue (Canon) from 'Pieces deClavecin';* **Dalza** *Pavana alla Venetiana (from Petrucci, 'Intabulatura de Lauto,' 1508);* **J.K.F. Fischer** Musikalischer Parnassus, 1738 - 'Thalia' Suite: *Gigue;* **Frescobaldi** Diverse curiose e rarissime partite (printed 1695): *Corrente;* **Froberger** Diverse curiose e rarissime partite (printed 1695): *Courante;* **Gervaise** 'Danseries,' 1550/1555: *Pavane d'Angleterre;* **Kindermann** *Ballet;* **J. Krieger** *Sarabande;* **Kuhnau** Neue Clavierübung II, 1692: *Gavotte;* **Monteverdi** Orpheo (1607): *'Moresca';* **Normiger** Tabulaturbuch of Christian, Duke of Windsor, 1598: *Der Mohren Aufzug (The Moor's Procession);* **Philips** The Fitzwilliam Virginal Book: *Galliardo*

Echoes of Time (2-CD Set) MMO CD 3357
Agricola, Alexander Fridolin Sicher's 'Ein Altes Spielbuch', c. 1500: *Fors seulement;* **Brumel** *Vray dieu d'amours (from Fridolin Sicher's 'Ein Altes Spielbuch', c. 1500);* **Compère** *Barises moy;* Fridolin Sicher's 'Ein Altes Spielbuch', c. 1500: *Se meuix;* **Isaac** Fridolin Sicher's 'Ein Altes Spielbuch', c. 1500: *E qui le dira; La mi la sol;* **Obrecht** Fridolin Sicher's 'Ein Altes Spielbuch', c. 1500: *Stat ein meskin was junck; Fors seulement; Fors seulement;* **Okeghem** Fridolin Sicher's 'Ein Altes Spielbuch', c. 1500: *Malor me bat; Fors seulement;* **des Pres** Fridolin Sicher's 'Ein Altes Spielbuch', c. 1500: *Cela sans plus;* **Susato** Het derde musyck boexken ('The Third Little Music Book') (Antwerp, 1551): *1. La bataillo; 02. Mille regretz ('Dittre Reue'), 03. Galliard le tout ('Das Ganze'); 04. Hoboecken dans ('Hoboeckentanz'); 05. Quatre branles ('Die vier Branlen'); 06. Pour quoy ('Warum'); 07. Mon amy ('Mein Freund'); 08. Ronde 6 & Saltarelle ('Hupfaut'); 09. Dont vient cela ('Woher kommt's') (basse danse); 10. Reprise ('Nachtanz') (basse danse); 11. Bergerette ('Schafertanz') (basse danse); 12. Mon desir ('Mein Verlangen') (basse danse); 13. Bergerette sans roch ('Ohne Fels') (basse danse) & Reprise ('Nachtanz'); 14. Danse du Roy ('Konigstanz') (basse danse) & Reprise ('Nachtanz'); 15. La mourisque ('Mohrentanz') (basse danse)*

Eighteenth Century Recorder Music (2-CD Set) MMO CD 3358
Loeillet *Sonata in F major;* **Sammartini** *Sonata No. 9 in G major; Sonata No. 11 in F major;* **Telemann** *Trio in G minor; Trio in F major*

English Consort Music (2-CD Set) MMO CD 3359
Brade *Canzon;* **Byrd** *Leaves Be Green, The;* **Cooperario** *Fantasia in C major;* **Dowland** Dances from 'Lachrimae': *1. Semper Dowland Semper Dolens; 2. The King of Denmark's Galiard; 3. The Earl of Essex Galiard; 4. M. Henry Noel His Galiard; 5. M. Giles Hobies Galiard; 6. M. Nicholas Gryffith His Galiard; 7. M. Thomas Collier His Galiard; 8. Captain Digorie Piper His Galiard; 9. M. Bucton's Galiard; 10. Mrs. Nichols Almand; 11. M. George Whitehead His Almand;* **Lawes** Consort Suite in G minor: *Fantasia; On the Plainsong; Air;* **Schein** Suite No. 3: *Pavane, Gagliarde, Courante; Allemande and tripla;* **Woodcock** *Browning 'Fantasy'*

Flute & Guitar Duets, vol. I (2-CD Set) MMO CD 3319
Anonymous *Green Sleeves to a Ground; Faronell's Ground;* **J.S. Bach** *Sonata in C major, BWV1033;* **E.G. Baron** *Sonata in G major;* **Couperin** *Sœur Monique;* **Dowland** *If My Complaints;* **Finger** *Division on a Ground;* **Pilkington** *Rest Sweet Nymphs;* **Vivaldi** *Andante (arranged from the Flute Concerto in G major, RV438)*

Flute & Guitar Duets, vol. II (3-CD Set) MMO CD 3320
Fauré Pelleas et Melisande: *Sicilienne;* **Giuliani** *Grand Duo Concertant (Sonata) for Flute and Guitar, op. 85;* **Ibert** *Entr'acte;* **Schubert** *An die Musik, op. 88, no. 4, D547;* **Villa-Lobos** *Bachianas Brasileiras No. 5; Distribution of the Flowers (Distribucao de Flores)*

HÄNDEL 3 Sonatas; TELEMANN 3 Duet Sonatas (2 Flutes) (2-CD Set) MMO CD 3343
Händel *Sonata for Flute and Piano in G major, op. 1, no. 5, HWV363b; Sonata for Flute (or recorder) and Piano in F major, op. 1, no. 11, HWV369; Sonata for Flute and Piano in E minor, op. 1, no. 1b, HWV359b;* **Telemann** *Duet Sonata No. 1 in D major; Duet Sonata No. 2 in G major; Duet Sonata No. 3 in A major*

HANDEL; MARCELLO; TELEMANN 3 Sonatas in F (Flute, harpsichord and viola da gamba) MMO CD 3350
Händel *Sonata in F major;* **B. Marcello** *Sonata in F major, op. 2, no. 1;* **Telemann** *Sonata in F major*

HAYDN 4 'London' Trios, HobIV:1-4 MMO CD 3309
'London' Trios: *No. 1 in C major, HobIV/1; No. 2 in G major, HobIV/2; No. 3 in G major, HobIV/3; No. 4 in G major, HobIV/4*

HAYDN Piano Trios, vol. I *F, D & G (HobXV:15-17)* MMO CD 3363
Trio in F major, HobXV/17; Trio in D major, HobXV/16; Trio in G major, HobXV/15

KUHLAU Trio in E-flat; BACH Sonatas in E-flat and A (2-CD Set) MMO CD 3345
Flute Sonata No. 2 in E-flat major, BWV1031; Flute Sonata No. 3 in A major, BWV1032; Trio for Three Flutes No. 3 in E-flat major, op. 86

MOZART Quartet in F, KV370 (KV368b); STAMITZ Quartet in F, op. 8, no. 3 MMO CD 3308

MOZART 3 Flute Quartets in D (KV285), C (KV285b/Anh.171) and A (KV298) MMO CD 3311

PEPUSCH Sonata in C; TELEMANN Sonata in C minor MMO CD 3346

PIAZZOLLA Histoire du Tango & other Latin Classics for Flute & Guitar Duet MMO CD 3364
Granados (arr. Reichert & Bury) Spanish Dances, op. 37, H142: *5. Andaluza (Playera);* **Piazzolla** Histoire du Tango: *1. Bordel 1900; 2. Café; 3. Nightclub; 4. Concert d'aujourd'hui;* **Sarasate** *Romanza Andaluza; Playera*

QUANTZ Trio Sonata in C minor; BACH Gigue; ABEL Sonata No. 2 in F MMO CD 3347

Renaissance Dances and Fantasias MMO CD 3356
Attaingnant Six Pavanes and Gaillardes from 1529: *1. Pavane 1; 2. Gaillarde 1; 3. Pavane 2; 4. Gaillarde 2; 5. Pavane 3; 6. Gaillarde 3; 7. Pavane 4; 8. Gaillarde 4; 9. Pavane 5; 10. Gaillarde 5; 11. Pavane 6; 12. Gaillarde 6;* **Banchieri** Fantasie overo canzoni alla Francese: *1. Fantasia prima; 2. Fantasia quarta; 3. Fantasia sesta; 4. Fantasia terza decima; 5. Fantasia decima quarta; 6. Fantasia decima settima; 7. Fantasia decima ottava; 8. Fantasia decima nona; 9. Fantasia vigesima; 10. Fantasia vigesimo prima;* **Praetorius** Dances from 'Terpsichore': *1. La Bouree; 2. Ballet des Amazones; 3. Branle; 4. Courante 1; 5. Courante 2; 6. Pavane de Spaigne; 7. Gaillarde; 8. Volte*

Romantic Classics for Flute & Piano (2-CD Set) MMO CD 3371
Debussy *Le Petit Berger; Le Petit Nègre;* **Donjon** *Pan (Pastorale);* **Fauré** *Berceuse, op. 16;* **M.A. Reichert** *Mélodie, op. 16; Rêverie, op. 17; Souvenir du Para, op. 10;* **Schubert** Schwanengesang, D957: *10. Das Fischermädchen;* Die Winterreise, op. 89, D911: *1. Gute Nacht;* **Schubert** Schwanengesang, D957: *4. Ständchen;* **Schumann, Robert** 3 Romanzen, op. 94: *'Nicht schnell'; 'Einfach, innig'*

TELEMANN & HANDEL - 3 Sonatas for Alto Recorder, Harpsichord & Viola da gamba MMO CD 3340
Händel *Sonata No. 3 in C major;* **Telemann** *Trio in F major; Trio Sonata in B-flat major*

TELEMANN Concerto No. 1 in D major/ CORRETTE Sonata in E minor MMO CD 3348

TELEMANN Trio in F major; B-flat major; HANDEL Sonata No. 3 in C major MMO CD 3349

3 Sonatas for Alto Recorder or flute or violin, Harpsichord & Viola da gamba (Händel, Telemann & Marcello) MMO CD 3341
Händel *Sonata in F major;* **B. Marcello** *Sonata in F major, op. 2, no. 1;* **Telemann** *Sonata in F major*

VERACINI Four Sonatas for Flute, Alto/Treble Recorder or Violin with Harpsichord MMO CD 3370
Sonata No. 1 in F major for Flute/Recorder or Violin with Harpsichord; Sonata No. 4 in B-flat major for Flute/Recorder or Violin with Harpsichord; Sonata No. 11 in F major for Flute/Recorder or Violin with Harpsichord; Sonata No. 12 in C minor for Flute/Recorder or Violin with Harpsichord

Woodwind Quintets, vol. I *The Joy of Woodwind Music* MMO CD 3335
Barthe Passacaille: *Passacaille;* **Beethoven** *Quintet (adapted from sextet, op. 71);* **Colomer** *Bourée;* **Haydn** *Minuet (Allegretto); Rondo (Presto);* **Lefebvre** Suite for Winds, op. 57: *III. Finale - Allegro leggiero;* **Mozart** *German Dance;* **A. Reicha** *Quintet in E-flat major, op. 88, no. 2*

Woodwind Quintets, vol. II *Jewels for Woodwind Quintet* MMO CD 3336
C.P.E. Bach *Andante (excerpt);* **J.S. Bach** Das Orgelbüchlein: *In Dulci Jubilo, BWV729 (chorale);* **Balay** *Petite Suite Miniature (I. Menuet; II. Courte Gavotte; III. Sarabande, IV. Petit Rondeau);* **Colomer** *Menuet;* **Danzi** *Quintet in G minor, op. 56, no. 2;* **Deslandres** Trois Pieces en Quintette: *Allegro;* **Haydn** *Introduction & Allegro; Octet (Menuetto & Trio);* **Klughardt** Quintet, op. 79: *Andante grazioso;* **Koepke** *Rustic Holiday;* **Mozart** *Minuet, KV421;* Divertimento No. 14, V270: *Allegro molto;* Divertimento No. 8, KV213: *Andante & Contradanse*

Inspirational

Christmas Memories MMO CDG 1203
O Holy Night; O Come, O Come, Emmanuel; Silent Night; Joy to the World; Jingle Bells; O Come, All Ye Faithful; O Little Town of Bethlehem; Hark! The Herald Angels Sing; It Came Upon a Midnight Clear; The Twelve Days of Christmas; Auld Lang Syle

Instrumental Classics with Orchestra

J.S. BACH Brandenburg Concerti Nos. 4 in G major (BWV1049) & 5 in D major (BWV1050) (2-CD Set) MMO CD 3310

J.S. BACH Brandenburg Concerto No. 2 in F; HAYDN Concerto in D, HobVII/1 MMO CD 3306

J.S. BACH Suite No. 2 for Flute & Strings in B minor, BWV1067(2-CD Set) MMO CD 3302

J.S. BACH 'Triple' Concerto in A minor, BWV1044; VIVALDI Concerto in D minor, op. 8, no. 9, RV236 MMO CD 3307

Band Aids *Concert Band Favorites with Orchestra* MMO CD 3352
J.S. Bach *Chorale No. 42; Chorale No. 297;* **Beethoven** *Variations on a Theme by Paisiello; Contradanse;* The Ruins of Athens, op. 113: *Turkish March;* **Brahms** *A Melody Is Drifting;* **Dvorak** *Slavonic Dance;* **D. Gabrielli** Sacre Symphoniae: *Canzon;* **Haydn** String Quartet in C major, 'Emperor,' op. 76, no. 3, HobIII/77: *II. Andante;* **Lully** *Minuet;* **Palestrina** Te Deum Landamus (Mass): *Crucifixus;* **Prokofiev** The Love for Three Oranges: *March;* **Smetana** The Bartered Bride (Prodana Nevesta): *Polka;* **Sullivan** *There Lived a King;* **Tchaikovsky** Romeo and Juliet: *Theme;* **Trad. (Hymn)** *Christ the Lord Is Risen Today*

BOCCHERINI Concerto in D major; VIVALDI Concerto No. 2 in G minor 'La Notte'; MOZART Andante for Flute and Strings MMO CD 3303

Concert Band Favorites with Orchestra MMO CD 3351
J.S. Bach *Sarabande;* **Bizet** Carmen: *Toreador Song;* **Chopin** *Prelude, op. 28, no. 7;* **Dittersdorf** *Tournament of Temperaments (The Melancholic, The Humble, The Gentle);* **MacDowell** *To a Wild Rose;* **Mendelssohn** *Solemn March;* **Schubert** *Moment Musical, op. 94, D780, no. 3;* **Schumann** Kinderszenen, op. 15: *7. Träumerei;* **Verdi** Aïda: *Triumphal March*

First Chair Solos with Orchestral Accompaniment MMO CD 3333
Bizet Carmen - Act III: *Introduction;* **Händel** *Gigue; Minuet No. 2;* The Water Music, HWV348: *Minuet No. 2;* **Haydn** Symphony No. 101, 'The Clock': *II. Maggiore; III. Minuet;* Symphony No. 90: *II. Andante;* **Mendelssohn** Hebrides Overture, op. 26: *Fingal's Cave;* A Midsummer Night's Dream, op. 61: *excerpt (Scherzo);* **Mozart** *Allegretto - Trio;* Divertimento, KV131: *Menuetto;* **Rossini** William Tell: *Overture;* **Tchaikovsky** The Nutcracker: *'Chinese Dance'; 'Dance of the Mirlitons'*

HAYDN Divertimento in D major; VIVALDI Concerto in D major, op. 10 No. 3 'Bullfinch'; FREDERICK THE GREAT Concerto in C major MMO CD 3304

MOZART Concerto for Flute & Harp in C major, KV299 (3-CD Set) MMO CD 3361

MOZART Concerto No. 1 in G major, KV313 (KV285c) (2-CD Set) MMO CD 3301

MOZART Concerto No. 2 in D major, KV314 (KV285d); QUANTZ Concerto in G major (2-CD Set) MMO CD 3362

TELEMANN Suite A minor; GLUCK 'Orpheus' scene; PERGOLESI Concerto G major (2-CD Set) MMO CD 3312
Orfeo ed Euridice: *scene for Flute & Orchestra; Flute Concerto in G major; Suite in A minor for Flute & Orchestra*

VIVALDI Concerti in D major (RV427); F major (RV434); G major (RV438) MMO CD 3314

VIVALDI Concerti in D major (RV429); G major (RV435); A minor (RV440) MMO CD 3315

VIVALDI Concerto in F major, op. 10, no. 1, RV433 'La Tempesta di Mare'; TELEMANN Concerto in D major; LECLAIR Concerto in C major (2-CD Set) MMO CD 3305
Flute Concerto in C major; Flute Concerto in D major; Flute Concerto in F major, op. 10, no. 1, RV433 'La Tempesta di Mare'

Laureate Master Classes with Piano

Beginning Flute Solos, vol. I (Murray Panitz)   MMO CD 3321
Gretchaninov *First Waltz;* Hopkins *Wanton Waltz; Flirtations Fancy;* Lewallen *Poeme Petite;* Lully (transcr. Felix) *Dances for the King (Bourree & Minuet; Sarabande; Gavotte);* Mozart (transcr. Lentz) *Quartet for Flute and Strings in D major, KV285: Adagio;* Schubert (arr. Isaac) *Three Themes (Melody from Octet, op. 166; Lullaby; The Rosamunde Air): Three Themes (Melody from Octet, op. 166; Lullaby; The Rosamunde Air)*

Beginning Flute Solos, vol. II (Donald Peck)   MMO CD 3322
Gossec *Gavotte;* Hindemith *Echo;* Kuhlau *Menuett;* Lewallen *Andantino;* Marpurg (arr. Scarmolin) *Rondo;* Sumerlin *Serenade;* Tailleferre *Pastorale*

Beginning Flute Solos, vol. III (Doriot Anthony Dwyer)   MMO CD 3330
Bartók *Evening in the Country;* Berlioz *The Damnation of Faust, op. 24: Three Songs ('King of Thule'; 'Mephistoheles' Serenade'; 'Faust's Air');* Fauré *En Prière;* Ibert *Histoires (Crystal Cage, Leader of the gold Tortoise, and Little White Donkey): Histoires (Crystal Cage, Leader of the gold Tortoise, and Little White Donkey);* Sibelius *Nocturne*

Intermediate Flute Solos, vol. I (Julius Baker)   MMO CD 3323
Händel *Sonata No. 5 in F major (I. Larghetto; II. Allegro; III. Siciliana; IV. Giga);* Pessard *Andalouse, op. 20;* Telemann *Sonata No. 7 in C minor: I. Allegro*

Intermediate Flute Solos, vol. II (Donald Peck)   MMO CD 3324
J.S. Bach *Suite in B minor: Polonaise & Bardinerie;* Baksa *Aria da Capo;* A. Marcello *Flute Sonata in F major: I. Adagio (Andantino); II. Largo; III. Allegro;* Widor *Scherzo*

Intermediate Flute Solos, vol. III (Donald Peck)   MMO CD 3327
Joachim Andersen *Scherzino, op. 55, no. 6 (normal tempo and slow practice tempo);* Gluck *Minuet and Dance of the Blessed Spirits;* Händel *Flute Sonata No. 2 in G major, op. 1, no. 5, HWV363b: I. Adagio; II. Allegro;* R. Lane *Flute Sonata: I. Allegro vivace (normal tempo and slow practice tempo);* Mozart *Andante in C major, KV285e (KV315)*

Intermediate Flute Solos, vol. IV (Doriot Anthony Dwyer)   MMO CD 3331
Avschalomov *Disconsolate Muse;* Haydn *Symphony No. 24: Adagio;* Martinon *Sonatine;* Mendelssohn *Song without Words, op. 62, no. 1; Song without Words, op. 102, no. 3*

Advanced Flute Solos, vol. I (Murray Panitz)   MMO CD 3325
J.S. Bach *Flute Sonata No. 2 in E-flat major, BWV1031: I. & II. (1st & 2nd movements);* Hindemith *Flute Sonata: I. Heiter bewegt;* Mozart (arr. Leeuwen) *Flute Concerto No. 2 in D major, KV314 (KV285d): I. Allegro aperto (excerpt)*

Advanced Flute Solos, vol. II (Julius Baker)   MMO CD 3326
J.S. Bach (ed. Rampal) *Flute Sonata No. 7 in G minor: I. Allegro moderato;* Fauré *Fantaisie, op. 79;* Mozart *Flute Concerto No. 1 in G major, KV313 (KV285c): I. Allegro maestoso*

Advanced Flute Solos, vol. III (Murray Panitz)   MMO CD 3328
Händel *Sonata No. 2 in G minor: I. Adagio; IV. Presto;* Henze *Sonatine: I. Moderato;* Quantz (rev. Wumer) *Flute Concerto in G major: I. Allegro;* Telemann (transcr. Wummer) *Suite in A minor: II. 'Les Plaisirs'*

Advanced Flute Solos, vol. IV (Julius Baker)   MMO CD 3329
J.S. Bach (arr. Barrere) *Cantata No. 156, BWV156: Arioso;* Fauré (arr. Cavally) *Pelleas et Melisande: Sicilienne;* Godard (arr. Cavally) *Idylle, op. 116;* Platti (arr. Moyse) *Sonata No. 2 in G major: Adagio; IV. Allegro molto*

Advanced Flute Solos, vol. V (Doriot Anthony Dwyer)   MMO CD 3332
Dutilleux *Sonatine for Flute;* Piston *Flute Sonata*

Pop, Blues & Jazz Classics

BOLLING Suite for Flute and Jazz Piano Trio   MMO CD 3342
Suite for Flute & Jazz Piano Trio: *Baroque and Blue; Sentimentale; Javanaise; Fugace; Irlandaise; Veratile; Véloce*

Classic Rags for Flute and Piano   MMO CD 3372
The Birds' Carnival; Blue Goose; The Entertainer; Pine Apple Rag; Solace; Gladiolus Rag; Ragtime Nightingale; Ragtime Oriole; Echo of Spring

Student Series

Classic Themes for Students, 27 Easy Songs (2nd-3rd year)   MMO CD 3355
Albéniz *Tango;* Cohan *Little Johnny Jones: The Yankee Doodle Boy;* Curtis *Come Back to Sorrento;* Donato *A Media Luz;* Dvorak *Humoresque No. 7, op. 101, no. 7; Slavonic Dance;* Foster *Beautiful Dreamer;* Händel *Xerxes (Serse), HWV40: Largo;* Ivanovici *Waves of the Danube;* Key *The Star Spangled Banner;* Lehár *Gold and Silver (waltz);* Lemare *Andantino;* Leybach *Fifth Nocturne;* Offenbach *Apache Dance; Les Contes d'Hoffmann (Tales of Hoffman): Barcarolle (Moderato);* Pestalozza *Ciribiribin;* Rubinstein *Melody in F, op. 3, no. 1;* Schubert *Moment Musical; Ellens Gesang III: 'Ave Maria', op. 52, no. 6;* J. Strauss, Jr. *Blue Danube (waltz); Tales from the Vienna Woods;* Tchalkovsky *None but the Lonely Heart (Nur wer die Sehnsucht kennt), op. 6, no. 6;* Trad. (English folk song) *Country Gardens (English folk song);* Trad. (Gypsy melody) *Two Guitars;* Trad. (Gypsy song) *Dark Eyes;* Trad. (Scottish song) *Loch Lomond;* Wagner *Tannhäuser, WWV70: Evening Star*

Easy Flute Solos   *Beginning Students, vol. I* (2-CD Set)   MMO CD 3316
Stephen Adams *The Holy City;* Beethoven *Für Elise;* di Capua *'O Sole Mio!;* Chiara *La Spagnola;* Chopin *Fantaisie Impromptu, op. 66 (theme);* Clay *I'll Sing Thee Songs of Araby;* Crouch *Kathleen Mavourneen;* Dacre *Daisy Bell (A Bicycle Built for Two);* d'Hardelot *Because;* Elgar *Pomp and Circumstance;* Fearis *Beautiful Isle of Somewhere;* Harris *After the Ball;* Herbert *Serenade; The Fortune Teller: Gypsy Love Song;* Howe *Battle Hymn of the Republic;* Jacobs-Bond *I Love You Truly;* Jacobs-Bond (m); Stanton (l) *Just A-wearyin' for You;* Koven *O Promise Me;* Lehár *Die Lustige Witwe (The Merry Widow): 'Vilja';* Lincke *The Glow Worm;* MacDowell *To a Wild Rose;* Meacham *American Patrol;* Nevin *Mighty Lak' a Rose; The Rosary;* Nugent *Sweet Rosie O'Grady;* Partichella *Mexican Hat Dance;* Rachmaninov *Piano Concerto No. 2 in C minor, op. 18 (Theme);* Rimsky-Korsakov *Song of India;* Rodrigues *La Cumparsita;* C. Sanders *Adios Muchachos;* Schubert *Who Is Sylvia?;* Sibelius *Finlandia;* Tchaikovsky *Marche Slave;* Trad. (American cowboy song) *Red River Valley;* Trad. (Hebrew melody) *Eili, Eili;* Trad. (Hebrew national anthem) *Hatikvoh (The Hope);* Trad. (Neapolitan song) *Santa Lucia;* Trotère *In Old Madrid;* Villoldo *El Choclo;* Ward, Charles E. *The Band Played On;* Ward, Samuel A. (m); Bates, Katharine Lee (l) *America, the Beautiful;* Yradier (Iradier) *La Paloma*

Easy Flute Solos   *Beginning Students, vol. II* (2-CD Set)   MMO CD 3317
Jay Arnold *Blues in E-flat;* J.S. Bach *Jesu, Joy of Man's Desiring; Chorale No. 83; Das Orgelbüchlein: In Dulci Jubilo, BWV729 (chorale);* Bizet *Carmen: Toreador Song;* Borodin *Prince Igor: Melody (Moderato);* Brahms *Cradle Song;* Daniels *You Tell Me Your Dream;* Lawlor *The Sidewalks of New York: The Sidewalks of New York;* Mendelssohn *Nocturne;* Offenbach *Bluebeard (scene);* Prokofiev *Peter and the Wolf, op. 67;* Rimsky-Korsakov *The Young Prince and the Young Princess;* Scheherazade, op. 35;* Schubert *Valse Noble, op. 77, D969;* Smetana *The Moldau (theme);* Sousa *The High School Cadets; Manhattan Beach; The Rifle Regiment; The Stars & Stripes Forever;* J. Strauss, Jr. *Der Zigeunerbaron (The Gypsy Baron): Recruiting Song;* Josef Strauss *Fireproof Polka;* Stravinsky *l'Oiseau de Feu (The Firebird): Berceuse; excerpt;* Trad. *I Ain't Gonna Study War No More; On Top of Old Smoky; Mr. Frog Went a'Courtin'!; When I Was Single; Old Paint; Careless Love; When the Saints Go Marching In;* Trad. (college song) *Spanish Guitar;* Trad. (English folk song) *Greensleeves;* Trad. (Folk song) *Black Is the Color of My True Love's Hair;* Trad. (Russian folk song) *The Cossack*

Easy Jazz Duets   *Two Flutes and Rhythm Section*   MMO CD 3318
The Green Danube; Tone Colors; Reaching Up; Uptown-Downtown; Main Street; Ski Slope; Doing Your Chores; Stop and Go; Glider; Jumper; Da Dit; Hot Fudge; Tijuana; La De Da De; Switcheroo; Swing Easy; Hop Scotch; Swingin' in the Rain; 4/4 Waltz; One Note Break; Lazy; Bits and Pieces

Flute Song   *Easy Familiar Classics with Orchestra*   MMO CD 3313
J.S. Bach *Orchestral Suite No. 3 in D major, BWV1068: Air on a 'G String';* Beethoven *Minuet in G major, WoO10/2;* Brahms *Hungarian Dance No. 5 in G minor, WoO1/5;* Dvorak *Humoresque No. 7, op. 101, no. 7;* Godard *Jocelyn: Berceuse;* Mozart *Divertimento No. 17 in D major, KV320b (KV334): Minuet;* Raff *Cavatine, op. 85, no. 3;* Schubert *Serenata (adapted from 'Schwanengesang,' D957, no. 4: 'Ständchen');* Schumann *Kinderszenen, op. 15: 7. Träumerei*

Teacher's Partner   *Basic Flute Studies, first year*   MMO CD 3334
Flute Tuning Instructions; Play from C to G and Back; F-major scale (using whole notes; then quarter notes; then half notes); G-major scale (using half notes; then quarter notes/rests; then using eighth notes); C-major scale (using dotted whole notes; then quarter, sixteenth and eighth notes); B-flat-major scale (using whole notes; then using sixteenth notes); A-flat-major scale (using a half, quarter and two eighth notes; then using a quarter note and two eighths); Octave Skips; Scale Cycle (5 scales); Courtly Dance (solo in C major); Solitude (solo in F major); Perky Miss (duet in F major); March of the Toys (solo in G major); Graceful Partners (duet in G major); Burlesca (solo in C major); Wistful Dream (duet in C major); Go, Go West (solo in B-flat major); Igor Centric (duet in B-flat major); Romance (solo in A-flat major); Canon in A-flat major (duet); French Waltz (duet); Flute Graduation Piece

World Favorites   *Student Editions, 41 Easy Selections (1st-2nd year)*   MMO CD 3354
Balfe *Then You'll Remember Me;* Becucci *Tesoro Mio;* di Capua *'O Sole Mio!;* Chopin *Etude, op. 10, no. 3;* Daly *Chicken Reel;* Debussy *Clair de Lune;* d'Hardelot *Because;* Dresser *On the Banks of the Wabash;* Evans *In the Good Old Summertime;* Franck *Messe solennelle, op. 12, M61: 5. Panis Angelicus (O Lord Most Holy);* Gruber *Silent Night;* Herbert *Romany Life;* J.H. Hopkins *We Three Kings of Orient Are;* Jessel *Parade of the Tin Soldiers;* Kennedy *Star of the East;* Lehár *Die Lustige Witwe (The Merry Widow): The Merry Widow Waltz;* Lincke *The Glow Worm;* MacDowell *To a Wild Rose; To a Water Lily;* Marchetti *Fascination;* L. Mason *Nearer, My God, to Thee;* Mendelssohn *Hark, the Herald Angels Sing;* Murray *Away in a Manger/Silent Night;* Neidlinger, W.H. *The Birthday of a King;* Nevin *Mighty Lak' a Rose;* Olcott *My Wild Irish Rose;* Poulton *Aura Lee;* Reading *Come All Ye Faithful;* Spilman *Flow Gently, Sweet Afton;* Trad. *He's Got the Whole World in His Hands;* Trad. (American cowboy song) *The Yellow Rose of Texas; Red River Valley;* Trad. (English folk song) *Greensleeves;* Trad. (Folk song) *Black Is the Color of My True Love's Hair;* Trad. (Irish melody) *Londonderry Air;* Trad. (Irish song) *Sweet Molly Malone;* Trad. (Scottish song) *Blue Bells of Scotland;* Trad. (Spiritual) *Deep River;* Trad. (U.S. Army Song) *Caisson Song;* Trad. (U.S. Marine Corps Song) *The Marines' Hymn;* Trad. (Welsh song) *All through the Night;* Yradier (Iradier) *La Paloma*

To see our full flute catalogue, visit us on the web at

www.musicminusone.com

MUSIC MINUS ONE
50 Executive Boulevard
Elmsford, New York 10523-1325
800-669-7464 (U.S.)/914-592-1188 (International)

www.musicminusone.com
e-mail: mmogroup@musicminusone.com